FAMOUS SHIPWRECKS
ARCTIC OCEAN SHIPWRECKS

by Michelle Parkin

pogo

Ideas for Parents and Teachers

Pogo Books let children practice reading informational text while introducing them to nonfiction features such as headings, labels, sidebars, maps, and diagrams, as well as a table of contents, glossary, and index.

Carefully leveled text with a strong photo match offers early fluent readers the support they need to succeed.

Before Reading

- "Walk" through the book and point out the various nonfiction features. Ask the student what purpose each feature serves.

- Look at the glossary together. Read and discuss the words.

Read the Book

- Have the child read the book independently.

- Invite him or her to list questions that arise from reading.

After Reading

- Discuss the child's questions. Talk about how he or she might find answers to those questions.

- Prompt the child to think more. Ask: Why do ships sink in the Arctic Ocean? What are some ways to prevent this?

Pogo Books are published by Jump!
5357 Penn Avenue South
Minneapolis, MN 55419
www.jumplibrary.com

Library of Congress Cataloging-in-Publication Data

Names: Parkin, Michelle, 1984- author.
Title: Arctic Ocean shipwrecks / by Michelle Parkin.
Description: Minneapolis, MN: Jump!, Inc., [2024]
Series: Famous shipwrecks | Includes index.
Audience: Ages 7–10 years
Identifiers: LCCN 2023030107 (print)
LCCN 2023030108 (ebook)
ISBN 9798889966562 (hardcover)
ISBN 9798889966579 (paperback)
ISBN 9798889966586 (ebook)
Subjects: LCSH: Shipwrecks—Arctic Ocean—Juvenile literature.
Classification: LCC G525 .P364 2024 (print)
LCC G525 (ebook)
DDC 910.9163/2–dc23/eng/20230929
LC record available at https://lccn.loc.gov/2023030107
LC ebook record available at https://lccn.loc.gov/2023030108

Editor: Alyssa Sorenson
Designer: Anna Peterson

Photo Credits: Thierry Boyer, Parks Canada, cover, 10–11; mika_mgla/Shutterstock, 1; jo Crebbin/Shutterstock, 3; titoOnz/Shutterstock, 4; Maridav/Shutterstock, 5; Seemoregalery/Shutterstock, 6; mady70/Shutterstock, 7; Dino Osmic/Shutterstock, 8–9; U.S. Naval History and Heritage Command, 12–13; Reading Room 2020/Alamy, 14–15; Topical Press Agency/Getty, 16–17; Luis Leamus/Dreamstime, 18; Jeremy Potter/NOAA, 19; westphalia/iStock, 20–21; imageBROKER/Herbert Berger/Getty, 23.

Printed in the United States of America at Corporate Graphics in North Mankato, Minnesota.

TABLE OF CONTENTS

CHAPTER 1
Icy Ocean......................................4

CHAPTER 2
Lost at Sea....................................6

CHAPTER 3
Exploring the Arctic Today.............18

QUICK FACTS & TOOLS
Where They Sank in the Arctic.............22
Glossary....................................23
Index......................................24
To Learn More..............................24

CHAPTER 1

ICY OCEAN

Brrrr! Grab a jacket. We are heading to the Arctic! The Arctic Ocean is in the north. The North Pole is in its center. The ocean is surrounded by Greenland, **Eurasia**, and North America.

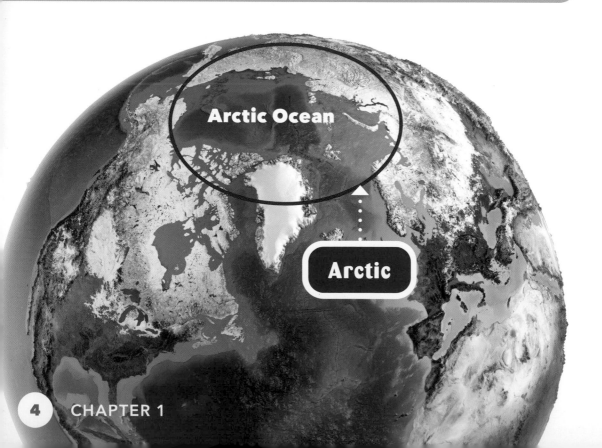

Arctic Ocean

Arctic

The Arctic Ocean's water is very cold. It has a lot of ice. It is cold above the water, too.

CHAPTER 2

LOST AT SEA

People have **explored** the Arctic for hundreds of years. But traveling through the ocean's icy water is dangerous. Many ships have gotten stuck. Some have even sunk.

The ship *Octavius* was traveling through the Arctic Ocean in 1762. It disappeared near Alaska. It was found 13 years later sailing near Greenland.

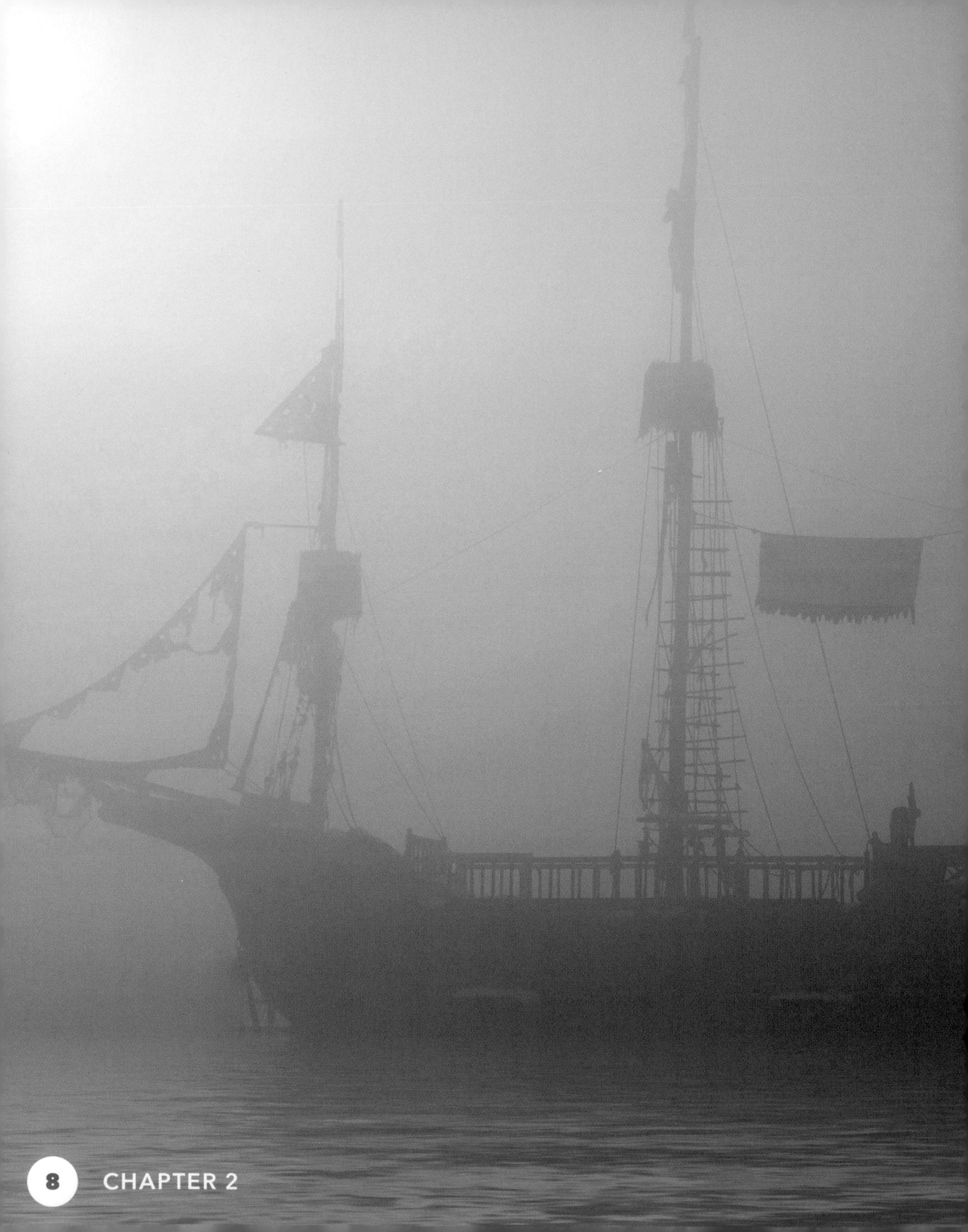

Octavius's **crew** was still on the ship! But they were all frozen solid. They did not survive the cold.

DID YOU KNOW?

When *Octavius* was found, people called it a ghost ship. Why? A ghost ship is a ship that sails without a crew.

It was September 1846. HMS *Erebus* and HMS *Terror* got stuck in Arctic ice. The crews went to a nearby island. They left the ships to look for help. Eventually, the ships sank.

The *Erebus* **shipwreck** was discovered in 2014. Two years later, *Terror* was found. Both ships are at the bottom of the ocean in northern Canada.

WHAT DO YOU THINK?

Erebus and *Terror* were found more than 160 years after they sank. Both shipwrecks were in good condition. Why do you think that is?

HMS
Erebus

TAKE A LOOK!

Damage from ice has caused ships to sink in the Arctic Ocean. How? Take a look!

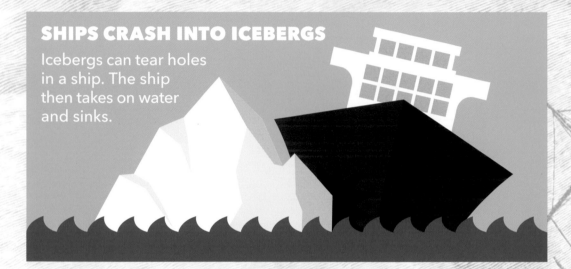

SHIPS CRASH INTO ICEBERGS

Icebergs can tear holes in a ship. The ship then takes on water and sinks.

FLOATING ICE CAN PUSH AGAINST A SHIP

Floating ice can trap a ship and damage it. The damage might cause the ship to sink.

USS *Jeannette* left California on July 8, 1879. It was going to the North Pole. In 1880, Arctic ice crushed the ship and damaged it. *Jeannette* started leaking. The crew tried to save it. But it sank near Russia in 1881. Only 13 people survived.

USS *Jeannette*

In August 1913, *Karluk* was near Alaska. It got stuck in thick ice. The ship and people on board were trapped for five months. Eventually, the ice ripped a long, large hole in the ship. Water rushed in. The ship sank.

WHAT DO YOU THINK?

Survivors on the *Karluk* waited a year to be **rescued** by another ship. What do you think that felt like for the survivors?

Karluk

SS *Terra Nova*

In 1943, the SS *Terra Nova* was sailing to Canada. But it hit ice. Water flooded the ship. It sank. The U.S. Coast Guard saved the crew.

In July 2012, a U.S. **research team** was exploring the ocean floor. They accidentally found the sunken ship!

CHAPTER 3
EXPLORING THE ARCTIC TODAY

Ships still travel through the Arctic Ocean. Some get stuck in ice. But radios help crews **contact** people on land.

ROV

Scientists study the ocean. They send **remotely operated vehicles (ROVs)** deep underwater. They map the ocean floor. Sometimes they find lost shipwrecks!

Icebreakers break up ice. They make safe paths for other ships. They also help ships that are stuck in ice.

There is still a lot to learn about the Arctic Ocean. People look for shipwrecks. Who knows what lost wreck will be found next?

icebreaker

QUICK FACTS & TOOLS

WHERE THEY SANK IN THE ARCTIC

① *Octavius** disappeared in 1762. It was found 13 years later near Greenland.

② HMS *Erebus* and HMS *Terror* got stuck in ice in 1846. The *Erebus* shipwreck was found in 2014. *Terror* was discovered in 2016.

③ USS *Jeannette* began its journey in 1879, but it was damaged by ice. It sank in 1881 near Russia.

④ *Karluk* got stuck in Arctic ice in 1913 near Alaska. It sank in January 1914.

⑤ SS *Terra Nova** sank in 1943 and was found in 2012.

*exact location unknown

GLOSSARY

contact: To communicate with someone.

crew: A group of people who work on a ship.

damage: Harm.

Eurasia: The mass of land that makes up Europe and Asia.

explored: Traveled and discovered things.

icebreakers: Ships designed to clear away ice in frozen waters so that other ships can pass through.

remotely operated vehicles (ROVs): Unmanned underwater machines used to explore deep ocean water.

rescued: Saved from a dangerous situation.

research team: A group of people that works together to collect information on something.

shipwreck: The remains of a sunken ship.

INDEX

crew 9, 10, 13, 17, 18

Erebus 10

Eurasia 4

explored 6, 17

ghost ship 9

Greenland 4, 7

ice 5, 6, 10, 12, 13, 14, 17, 18, 20

icebergs 12

icebreakers 20

Jeannette 13

Karluk 14

North America 4

North Pole 4, 13

Octavius 7, 9

radios 18

remotely operated vehicles (ROVs) 19

rescued 14

research team 17

stuck 6, 10, 14, 18, 20

Terra Nova 17

Terror 10

trapped 12, 14

U.S. Coast Guard 17

TO LEARN MORE

Finding more information is as easy as 1, 2, 3.

❶ Go to www.factsurfer.com

❷ Enter "ArcticOceanshipwrecks" into the search box.

❸ Choose your book to see a list of websites.

FACT SURFER